Michael and Eric Scra

MACHINE LEARNING BOOK PYTHON

The Perfect Handbook For Building A
Top-Notch Code In Scratch And
Using Python Data Science Programming To
Elevate Your Skills Out Of The Ordinary

Table of Contents

Introduction

Python is an incredibly easy computer programming language to learn and is also one of the most useful. Many of the biggest websites today are built with Python, and just to show how popular and powerful it really is, even NASA uses it. For starters, it's the best language for any computer coding beginner, giving you a great platform from which to move on to bigger and better things.

This will guide you step by step and show you everything you need to know in order to get started.

We could consider programming even easier than learning a new language because the programming language will be governed by a set of rules, which are, generally, always similar, so you could say that it might be considered as a natural language.

Thanks again for purchasing this book. I hope you enjoy it!

Chapter 1:

Introduction to Python

What is Python?

Python is an awesome decision on machine learning for a few reasons. Most importantly, it's a basic dialect at first glance. Regardless of whether you're not acquainted with Python, getting up to speed is snappy in the event that you, at any point, have utilized some other dialect with C-like grammar.

Second, Python has an incredible network, which results in great documentation and inviting and extensive answers in Stack Overflow (central!).

Third, coming from the colossal network, there are a lot of valuable libraries for Python (both as "batteries included" an outsider), which take care of essentially any issue that you can have (counting machine learning).

However, here's the caveat: libraries can and do offload the costly computations to the substantially more performant (yet much harder to use) C and C++ are prime examples. There's NumPy, which is a library for numerical calculation. It is composed in C, and it's quick. For all intents and purposes, each library out there that includes serious estimations utilizes it—every one of the libraries recorded next utilize it in some shape. On the off chance that you read NumPy, think quickly. In this way, you can influence your computer scripts to run essentially as quick as handwriting them out in a lower level dialect. So, there's truly nothing to stress over with regards to speed and agility. If you want to know which Python libraries, you should check out. Try some of these.

"Scikit-learn"

Do you need something that completely addresses everything from testing and training models to engineering techniques?

Then scikit-learn is your best solution. This incredible bit of free programming gives each device important to machine learning and information mining. It's the true standard library for machine learning in Python; suggested for the vast majority of the 'old' ML calculations.

This library does both characterization and relapse, supporting essentially every calculation out there (bolster vector machines, arbitrary timberland, Bayes, you name it). It allows a simple exchange of calculations in which experimentation is a lot simpler. These 'more seasoned' calculations are shockingly flexible and work extremely well in a considerable amount of problems and case studies.

In any case, that is not all! Scikit-learn additionally does groupings, plural dimensionalities, and so on. It's likewise exceedingly quick since it keeps running on NumPy and SciPy.

Look at a few cases to see everything this library is prepared to do, the instructional exercises on the website, and the need to figure out if this is a good fit.

"NLTK"

While not a machine learning library, essentially, NLTK is an unquestionable requirement when working with regular computer language. It is bundled with a heap of Datasets and other rhetorical data assets, which is invaluable for preparing certain models. Aside from the libraries for working with content, this is great for determining capacities, for example, characterization, tokenization, stemming, labeling, and parsing—that's just the beginning.

The handiness of having the majority of this stuff perfectly bundled can't be exaggerated. In case you are keen on regular computer language, look at a few of their website's instructional exercises!

"Theano"

Utilized generally in research and within the scholarly community, Theano is the granddad of all deeply profound learning systems. Since it is written in Python, it is firmly incorporated with NumPy. Theano enables you to make neural systems which are essential scientific articulations with multi-dimensional clusters. Theano handles this so you that you don't need to stress over the real usage of the math included.

It bolsters offloading figures to a considerably speedier GPU, which is an element that everybody underpins today, yet, back when they presented it, this wasn't the situation.

The library is extremely developed now and boasts an extensive variety of activities, which is extraordinary with regards to contrasting it and other comparative libraries.

The greatest grievance out there about Theano is the API might be cumbersome for a few, making the library difficult to use for beginning learners.

In any case, there are tools that relieve the agony and make working with Theano pretty straightforward; for example, try using Keras, or Blocks, and even Lasagne.

"TensorFlow"

The geniuses over at Google made TensorFlow for inside use in machine learning applications and publicly released it in late 2015. They needed something that could supplant their more established, non-open source machine learning structure, *DistBelief*. It wasn't sufficiently adaptable and too firmly ingrained into their foundation. It was to be imparted to different analysts around the globe.

Thus, TensorFlow was made. Despite their slip-ups in the past, many view this library as a much-needed change over Theano, asserting greater adaptability and more instinctive API. Another great benefit is it can be utilized to create new conditions, supporting tremendous amounts of new GPUs for training and learning purposes. While it doesn't bolster as wide a scope of functionality like Theano, it has better computational diagram representations.

TensorFlow is exceptionally famous these days. In fact, if you are familiar with every single library on this list, you can agree that there has been a huge influx in the number of new users and bloggers in this library and its functionality. This is definitely a good thing for beginners.

"Keras"

Keras is a phenomenal library that gives a top-level API to neural systems and is best for running alongside or on top of Theano or TensorFlow. It makes bridling the full intensity of these intricate bits of programming substantially simpler than utilizing them all by themselves. The greatest benefit of this library is its exceptional ease of understanding, putting the end-users' needs and experiences as its number one priority. This cuts down on a number of errors.

It is also secluded; which means that individual models like neural layers and cost capacities can be grouped together with little to no limitations. This additionally makes the library simple to include new models and interface them with the current ones.

A few people have called Keras great that it is similar to cheating on your exam. In case you're beginning with higher learning in this area, take the illustrations and examples and discover what you can do with it. Try exploring.

Furthermore, by chance that you need to START learning, it is recommended that you begin with their instructional exercises and see where you can go from that point.

Two comparative choices are Lasagne and Blocks; however, they just keep running on Theano. If you attempted Keras and have difficulty, perhaps, experiment with one of these contrasting options to check whether they work out for you.

"PyTorch"

If you are looking for a popular deep learning library, then look no further than Torch, which is written in the language called Lua. Facebook recently open-sourced a Python model of Torch and named it PyTorch, which allows you to easily use the exact same libraries that Torch uses, but from Python, instead of the original language, Lua. PyTorch is significantly easier for debugging because of one major difference between Theano, TensorFlow, and PyTorch. The older versions use allegorical computation while the newer does not. Allegorical computation is simply a way of saying that coding an operation, for example, 'a + b', will not be computed when that line is read. Before it is executed, it must be translated into what is called CUDA or C. This makes the debugging much harder to execute in Theano/TensorFlow since this error is more difficult to pinpoint with a specific line of code. It's basically harder to trace back to the source. Debugging is not one of this library's strongest features.

This is extremely beginner-friendly; as your learning increases, try some of their more advanced tutorials and examples.

History of Python

Python was invented in the later years of the 1980s. Guido van Rossum, the founder, started using the language in December 1989. He is Python's only known creator and his integral role in the growth and development of the language has earned him the nickname "Benevolent Dictator for Life." It was created to be the successor of the language known as ABC.

The next version that was released was Python 2.0, in October of the year 2000 and had significant upgrades and new highlights, including a cycle-distinguishing junk jockey and back up support for Unicode. It was most fortunate that this particular version made vast improvement procedures to the language turned out to be more straightforward and network sponsored.

Python 3.0, which initially started its existence as Py3K. Funny right? This version was rolled out in December of 2008 after a rigorous testing period. This particular version of Python was hard to roll back to previous compatible versions which are the most unfortunate. Yet, a significant number of its real highlights have been rolled back to versions 2.6 or 2.7 (Python), and rollouts of Python 3 which utilizes the two to three utilities that help to automate the interpretation of the Python script. Python 2.7's expiry date was originally supposed to be back in 2015, but for unidentifiable reasons, it was put off until the year 2020. It was known that there was a major concern about data being unable to roll back but roll FORWARD into the new version, Python 3. In 2017, Google declared that there would be work done on Python 2.7 to enhance execution under simultaneously running tasks.

Four Ways to Reverse Strings and Lists

You are going to have four different ways that you can reverse the order of your strings or lists, depending on what your end goal is. You are going to do this whenever it comes to fixing a mistake that you may have made or to get a different result than what you got in the first place.

Reversing the list within itself

With this method, you are going to be taking the list itself and changing it with a simple line of code.

Example

Sample line = [4, 2, 5]

Sample line. Reverse ()

Print (sample line)

-> [5, 3, 4]

Fairly straightforward right? All you are doing is studying the list that you have created in Python and flipping it around by reading it from the end of the line to the beginning.

Iterating within a loop

When you are iterating inside of a loop, you are still going to be reversing your list, but instead, you are going to be doing it inside of a loop which is going to cause your list to be printed out one element at a time.

Example

For object in reverse ([5, 6, 2]): print (objects)

1 -> 2

2 -> 6

3 -> 5

Reverse a string inside of a line

Whenever you modify a string inside of a line, you are going to get the same result that you have been getting with the other examples that you have seen in this chapter. However, if you do not have any objects inside of that string, then you are going to be getting a different result than what you may be expecting.

Example

 "Sample line" [: : -1]

Enil elpmaS

A little different correct? Well, that is alright because either way, you are getting the reversed order of your string in the line that it is occupying.

Reversing a string by using the slicing method

You have used slicing to slice the indexes for strings, lists, and tuples. But, you can also use that same method to reverse the order of a string.

 It is going to work the same way that you would slice an index, and you are still going to get the reverse order of the string that you have created.

The code is going to look similar to the code that you just used in method three.

[3, 1, 5] [: : -1]

Result: 5, 1, 3

So, no matter which way you use it, you are going to be getting the reverse order of your lines and strings when you use the reverse code.

It is going to depend on what you are trying to accomplish in order to determine which method is going to be right for you. You may want to practice each of these methods so that you are able to get familiar with them and understand how they work.

Advantages of Python

The Python language is incredibly diverse, and this is due to the features that provide Python with an edge over all the other languages. The main advantages of using Python include:

Third-Party Modules

PyPI, or the Python Package Index, has multiple third-party modules that allow Python to interact with many different platforms and other computer programming languages.

Support Libraries

Python contains a significant standard library which is home to string operations, Internet protocols, operating system interfaces and web service tools

. The library contains scripts for several high-use tasks in programming, and this significantly cuts down on the amount of code that needs to be written.

Community Driven Open Source Development

Because Python has been developed using an OSI-approved license, it is open-source, free for anyone to use and modify for distribution and can also be used for commercial purposes. Not only that, it is a community-driven development which uses mailing lists and hosting conferences to collaborate for code and to get the numerous modules that it contains.

Data Structures that are User-Friendly

Python contains dictionary and list data structures built-in to provide construction of data structures for runtime. Also, Python also includes the options for data-typing at a high level, cutting down on the support code needed.

Productivity and Speed

Because Python is a clean-cut object-oriented language, it has enhanced capabilities for process control and also has integrated a framework for unit testing and capabilities for text processing, all of which provide support for the productivity and speed of the language. Python is considered to be the most useful for building network applications that are complex and consist of many protocols.

What is Python Programming?

This is a programming language that is objected-oriented and of high level and uses semantics. It is a high level in terms of structures in data and a combination of dynamic typing and binding. This is what makes it attractive to be used for Rapid Application Development and for connecting different elements.

Python, with its simplicity and learning with ease, helps in reading the programming language, and that is why it reduces the cost to maintain the program. Python encourages the program modularity and code reuse; this is because it supports different packages and modules. The standard library and the Python interpreter can be found in binary form. It is not necessary to charge all the available platforms and can be distributed freely.

Most programmers love the Python program because they offer great productivity. The edit-test debug is a cycle that is fast and does not need any compilation process. It is easier to debug a Python program; it will not cause any segmentation fault. An exception is raised when an error is discovered by the interpreter. When the exception is not known by the program, the interpreter prints a trace. The debugger, on a level of sourcing, will allow being inspecting any variables. There will be a settling of breakpoints, arbitrary expressions, and stepping on the code at any time. The Python is what writes the debugger, the easier, and a quick debugging method and programs of adding prints on the source and statements.

Python is open-source; this means you can use them freely for any commercial applications. Python is programmed to work on UNIX, Windows, and Mac and can be transferred to Java. Python is a language that helps in scripting and helps in web applications for different content.

It is like Perl and Ruby. Python is helped by several imaging programs; users are able to create customized extensions. There are different web applications supporting Python API like Blender and GIMP.

This information given on Python programming is beneficial for both the newbies and the experienced ones. Most of the experienced programmers can easily learn and use Python. There is an easier way to install Python. Most distributors of

UNIX and Linux have the recent Python. That is the reason why most computers come already installed with Python. Before you start using Python, you need to know which IDEs and text editors' best work with Python. To get more help and information, you can peruse through introductory books and code samples.

The Python idea was discovered in 1980 after the ABC language. Python 2.0 was introduced; it had features like garbage collection and list comprehensions; which are used in reference cycle collection. When Python 3.0 was released in 2008, it brought about a complete language revision. Python is primarily used for developing software and webs, for mathematics and scripting systems. The latest version of Python is known a Python 3 while Python 2 is still popular. Python was developed to help in reading and similar aspects to different languages like English and emphasis on Mathematics.

A new line is used to complete a Python command, as opposed to other programming languages that normally use semi-colons. It depends on indentation, whitespace, and defining the scope.

How to use Python Programming

Before using Python, you first need to install and run it on your computer, and once you do that, you will be able to write your first program. Python is known as a programming platform that cuts across multiple platforms. You can use it on Linux, macOS, Windows, Java, and .NET machines freely and as an open-source. Most of the Linux and Mac machines come preinstalled even though on an outdated version. That is the main reason why you will need to install the latest and current version.

An easier way to run Python is by using Thonny IDE; this is because it is bundled with the latest version of Python. This is an advantage since you will not need to install it separately. To achieve all that, you can follow the simple steps below:

- First, you will need to download Thonny IDE.

- Then, run the installer in order to install it on your computer.

- Click on File option, then new. Save the file on .py extension, for instance, morning.py or file.py. You are allowed to use any name for the file, as long as it ends with .py. Write the Python code on the file before saving it.

- To run the file, click on RUN, the run current script. Alternatively, click on F5 in order to run it.

There is also an alternative to install Python separately; it does not involve installing and running Python on the computer. You will need to follow the listed steps below:

- Look for the latest version of Python and download it.

- The next step is to run the installer file in order to install Python

- When installing, look for Add Python to environment variables. This will ensure that Python is added to the environment variables, and that will enable you to run Python from any computer destination and part. You have the advantage to choose the path to install Python.

- When you complete the process of installing, you can now run Python.

There is also an alternative and immediate mode to run Python. When Python is installed, you will type Python on the command line; the interpreter will be in immediate mode. You can type Python code, and when you press enter, you will get the output. For instance, when you type 1 + 1 and then press enter, you will get the output as 2. You can use it as a calculator, and you quit the process, type quit, and then press enter.

The second way to do it is by running Python on the Integrated Development Environment. You can use any editing software in order to write the Python script file. All you need to do is to save it the extension .py, and it is considered a lot easier when you use an IDE. The IDE is a feature that has distinctive and useful features like file explorers, code hinting, and syntax checking and highlighting that a programmer can use for application development.

You need to remember that when you install Python, there is an IDE labeled IDLE that will also be installed. That is what you will use to run Python on the computer, and it is considered the best IDE for beginners. You will have an interactive Shell when IDLE is opened. This is the point where you can have a new file and ensure that you save it as a .py extension.

Who can use Python Programming?

There is a big challenge out there in choosing a programming language that you can use for your coding businesses. The bigger question is, which language are you supposed to learn? Python is a program that is easy to use, and there are known companies that use it. This is one of the reasons why you should adapt to its uses. This is also the reason why worldwide developers have taken advantage.

Google

Since the beginning of Python, Google has been its supporter. They choose Python because it was easy to maintain it, deploy, and faster in delivery. The first web-crawling spider used for Google was in Java 1.0. It was difficult to use and maintain, and they had to do it again on Python. Python is one of the main programming languages that Google uses, the others include Java, C++, and Go that are used for production. Python is an important part of Google. They have been using it for many years, and it remains a system that is evolving and grows. Many engineers that work for Google prefer using Python. They keep seeking engineers with Python skills.

Facebook

Production engineers that work for Facebook have a positive comment about Python. This has made Python among the top three programming languages after C++ and Hack. Facebook adopted Python because it is easy to use. With over 5000 services on Facebook, this is definitely the best programming language. The engineers do not need to maintain or write much coding, and this allows them to focus on live improvements. This is one of the reasons why Facebook infrastructure scales efficiently. Python is used for infrastructure management, for network switch setup, and for imaging.

Instagram

From 2016, engineers working for Instagram declared that they were running the biggest Django web framework that was entirely written in Python. The engineers stated that they like Python because of the simple way to use it and how practical it is. That is why the engineers have invested their resources and time in using Python in all their trades. In recent times, Instagram has moved their codes from Python 2.7 to Python 3.

Spotify

Spotify is a music-streaming platform that uses Python as its programing language for back end services and data analysis. The reason why Spotify decided to use Python is that they like the way it works in writing and in coding. Spotify will use its analytics in order to offer its users recommendations and suggestions. For the interpretation, Spotify uses Luigi that collaborates with Hadoop. The source will handle the libraries that work together. It will consolidate all the error logs and helps in troubleshooting and redeployment.

Quora

Before implementing their idea, Quora decided to use Python programming for their question and answer platform. The Quora founders decided to go for Python because it was easy to read and write it. For great performance, they implemented C++. Python is still considered because of the frameworks it has like Pylons and Django.

Netflix

Netflix uses Python programming language to help in data analysis from their servers. They also use that in coding and other Python applications. It uses Python in the Central Alert Gateway and tracking any security history and changes.

Dropbox

This cloud storage system uses Python for the desktop client. Their programs are coded in Python. They use different libraries for Windows and Mac. And the reason being it is not preinstalled on any Mac or Windows, and the Python version differs.

Reddit

Python programming language was used to implement Reddit. They choose Python because it has different versions of code libraries, and it was flexible to develop it.

What can you do with Python Programming?

There are numerous applications for Python programming, like machine learning, data science, and web development. In addition, other several projects can use Python skills:

- With Python programming, you are able to automate boring stuff; this is the best approach for beginners. It helps with spreadsheet updates and renaming files. When you get to master Python basics, then this is the best point to start with. With the information, you will be able to create dictionaries, web scraping, creating objects, and working on files.

- Python will help you stay on top of the prices that are set on Bitcoin. Bitcoin and cryptocurrency have become a popular investment; this is because of its price fluctuation. In order to know the right move in regards to Bitcoin, you will need to be alert on their prices. With Python, it is possible to create a price notification for Bitcoin. This is the best way to start on crypto and Python.

- When your intention and plan is to create a calculator, Python is the best programming language. You will be able to build back-end and front-end services, which are the best when it comes to deployment. It is important to create applications that users can easily use. If your interest is in UX and UI design, then Python has a graphical user interface that is easy to work with.

- Python is the best programming language to use when mining data from Twitter. With the influx of technology and the internet, it is easy to get data and information easily. Data analytics is a very important concept; it involves what people are talking about and their behavioral patterns. To get all the answers, Twitter is the best place to start with when your interest is in data analysis. There is a data-mining project on Twitter, and that is when your Python skills will come in handy.

- You will have the ability to create a Microblog with a flask. In recent times, most people have a blog. But again, it is not a bad idea to have your personal hub online. With Instagram and Twitter, microblogging has become a popular concept. With Python skills, you will be able to create your own microblog. When you are into web development, you do not need to be worried about knowing Flask. You can learn about it online and then move to Django, which helps in web applications on a large scale.

- With Python skills, it is possible to build a Blockchain. The main reason for the development of blockchain was financial technology, even though it is spreading to other industries. As of now, blockchains can be used for any type of transaction, like medical records or real estate. When you get to build one for yourself, you will understand it better. You need to remember that blockchain is not just for the individuals who are interested in crypto. When you build one, you will have a creative way for technology implementation to your own interest.

- You can bottle your Twitter feed with your Python skills, and this will help in web applications. You can create a simple web app that can help in navigation on your Twitter feed. You will not be using Flask, but rather Bottle, a low-dependency approach that is easy and quick to implement.

- There are PyGames that are easy to play with Python skills. You can use the skills to code several games and puzzles. With the Pygame library, it is easier to create your own games and developing it. It is an open and free source with computer graphics and sound libraries, and it helps in adding up interactive functions in the application. There are different games that can be used for library creation.

- With Python, it is possible to create something in relation to storytelling. Since the language is easy to use, that is why it creates a better environment for development and interaction.

Importance of Python Programming in the Economics

Most people ask if it is important for economists to learn any programming language. The answer is that it is important since they will use the skills to test and crush data sets. Most of the economist use Python as their main programming language to help with efficiency in order to run complex models. The idea of data analysis is used by other professionals, not only by data scientists. Economists learn how to code in order to enjoy the ability to handle bigger data software. Large data can now be handled in spreadsheets when you use the new systems and all that can be done in a shorter time. That is the main reason why economists are adapting to the Python programming language.

Big data is what is used by different people all over. It helps in coding and for market and business intelligence. More spectrums of solutions are created by tech individuals, and they are not just for data scientists. This is why many economists are using and learning programming languages. Economists have been adapting to Python at a slower rate since they did not mostly depend on the data as compared to data scientists. They have adapted to the programming languages because of its flexibility, the breadth of functionalities, development, speed in computing, and the ability to operate between different systems.

Economists will deal with data that is on both low and high frequency. This is because of the increase in digitization and computing. The modern economy brings about greater power in computing and data sources. Years back, coding was used for only back office works, unlike recent times when it is used for front functions, and that is the reason why the use of Python has increased.

Benefits of learning Python language

Python is a self-sufficient language with many tools, and once the programmer is aware of all the utilities of these tools, then it is a cakewalk for them.

It requires less coding to complete basic tasks, therefore, making it an economical language.

Working knowledge of Python can be a stepping stone for many in the programming field since the methodologies used in the language can be widely used in a range of applications.

It also serves as a solid foundation to branch out and learn other languages as well.

Programmers who have learned the skills of this language are in great demand by some top companies like Google, Instagram, Disney, etc.

Thus, we can say that Python is not only a scripting language but a full-blown programming language. Surveys have revealed that Python had the largest growth of job demand in the last couple of years. With Python's vast capabilities programmer has a higher prospect in the web development field. One can easily design websites and applications with Python. However, like any other language, it also has some disadvantages, and they are:

Disadvantages of Python language

Since it is an interpreted language, it has been observed that it is often slower in execution than other languages. Python is not compatible with many browsers and mobile computing.

Since the typing is dynamic, therefore, it requires more testing as the errors show up only during run time.

Now that we know about the pros and cons of Python let us see in comparison with a few popular languages as to how Python stands out amongst them. Python has been often compared to languages such as JavaScript, Java, Perl, Smalltalk, Tcl and C++. These comparisons can be enlightening to know the nuances of this language. However, in a practical environment, the choice of a programming language is typically dictated by terms such as availability, training, prior investment and of course the cost involved. Let us look at some comparisons which we have drawn with other languages: *Java*—The programs run under Python are 3-5 times shorter than Java programs. This is due to the high level and dynamic typing of the language. The syntactic support is built directly into the language. For example, if you want to print "hello world" in

Python one simply has to type: ***print ('hello world')*** whereas in Java the same command would be covered in 4 lines.

JavaScript—Unlike JavaScript, Python supports writing of large programs with better codes by using object-oriented programming *Perl*- Both languages have a different philosophy where Perl supports common application-oriented tasks such as report generation, file scanning etc., whereas Python supports common programming methods such as designing a data structure. It encourages programmers to write readable and maintainable codes.

Tcl—As compared to Python, Tcl is weak on data structures and execute codes which are much slower. It also lacks the feature of writing large scale programs.

Smalltalk—The standard library of Smalltalk is more defined whereas, in case of Python, it has more facilities for dealing with the World Wide Web realities such as email, FTP and HTML.

C++— Just like Java when compared to C++, the programming code is 5-10 times shorter. It is said that what a C++ programmer can finish in a year Python programmer can finish in two months.

Importance of Python Programming at the Workplace

Several benefits come with learning Python if you have not learned the language. There is no need to panic because Python is a program that is easy to learn and can be used to learn other programming languages. You will understand the importance of Python since it is adopted by different companies like Instagram, Disney, Nokia, IBM, Pinterest, and Google.

When you learn about Python, you will have the skills needed to succeed and make good money at it.

- Python programming language helps in developing prototypes, and the reason is that it is quick to learn and work with.

- Most of the data mining and automation rely on Python. The reason being that language is better for general tasks.

- With Python, you will get a better and productive environment for coding, unlike what most programming languages like Java and C++ will do. Most coders claim that with Python, they are better organized and productive when it comes to their work.

- Since Python is not complicated and any beginner can easily read, learn, and understand, this means that anyone can work with the programming language. All that you will need is patience and practice to excel with the language. Python helps most programmers and development in large-scale dimensions.

- Django is an open-source used in web development and application that is powered by Python. With Python, it is easier to improve the maintenance and readability of codes. Python helps in securing coding with updates and maintenance. The reason being it helps in developing quality in the software application. You will also be able to demonstrate all the concepts when using syntax rules. The quality that Python offers in terms of maintenance and readability makes it the best programming language. You can even use English keywords instead of punctuations.

- Python helps with multiple paradigms that help a programmer know what is relevant in the work environment and requirement. Since Python supports different paradigms in programming, it is capable of featuring different concepts that relate to functional programming. With Python, it is possible to develop a software application that is complicated and large.

- Python help in integrating with different operating systems and interpreting different codes. There is a possibility to redevelop this application without recompiling.

- Python is able to provide better results as compared to the other programming language because of its library that is robust and big. From the library, it is possible to select the best as per the requirements and add more functionality to that. The feature will prevent having any additional code writing.

- Python helps in simplifying any complicated software. This programming language helps in data analytics and visualization in any program that is developing. When you are familiar with Python, you get to complete complex solutions without putting in a lot of time.

How can you earn using Python Programming?

Blogging

Python programming helps in creating a blog, and the blog is used in making money. There are different types of blogging. You can specialize in programming as your niche in blogging. There are numerous ways to use your blog as a programmer.

This includes online coding, charging your premium content, and affiliate links. Ensure all your content is SEO friendly with the relevant keywords that are what is used in ranking your page. In addition, SEO optimization should be on both on and off page. You will be guaranteed traffic to the site.

Apps Development

Your programming skills will be beneficial when you develop an app and monetize it. This programming helps in attaining that. Ensure that you market your app and use the automatic coding apps that will help in creating the app in a few minutes. With a great marketing technique, you will be able to make money out of app development. In order to sell it, you need to launch it on the App store.

Freelancing

This is a situation whereby you offer your services online. You should ensure that you look for the available online platforms and what works for you. You will be able to work from your own work schedule and make money while doing that. Some of the genuine and known platforms include Guru, Freelancer, and Upwork. You can also pitch directly to clients and offer your programming services.

You can earn using your Python skills when you make a plugin

The other alternative has a theme on WordPress. The best way to do it is by developing many apps and smaller modules like themes and WordPress plugins. This is a great way to make money coding online. Most websites use WordPress, so if you can create WordPress plugins, you are assured of making a lot of money.

Another way is to be an online educator and start selling your online courses

All this is possible when you use your Python skills and do coding. Most people are adopting online courses where people who cannot attend classes can still learn. When you have a personal website, you can offer free courses and tutorials and have traffic. You can teach many students in economics and finance on how to code and Python skills.

When you join coding competitions, you will be using your Python skills and still earn some good money

You can do development, data science, and design. When you are a winner, you are paid and get access to big companies who are on the lookout for competent coders.

Your Python skills will help in website creation

You can share your programming tips and then display what you have. Ensure that your website shows all your skills, your bans, and your portfolio as a coder. When you have your brand established, you will get more clients that will be willing to get your services and consultation, and you can charge for that. A website can bring your earnings through Google Adsense, affiliate marketing, and sponsored ads.

Basic Concepts in Python Programming

The first step to learning Python programming is to make sure that you have understood the ways of learning the language. By understanding how to learn is the most critical skills needed in computer programming. The importance of knowing how to learn is that languages evolve, new libraries are created, and tools upgraded. You must be able to keep up with the changes to be successful in the programming world.

In the modern world, one of the most used languages is Python. This is not just a language, and it is a method of how to do things in a simple and the right way. It is a common high-level language used in open source. Python is a vast language, and the more you learn about Python, the more information you will need to learn. This is an ironic statement, but that's how it is. Python uses a simple object-oriented approach and high-level data structures. Pythons also use simple dynamic typing and syntax. Python is a language that is compact, fast, and can efficiently work in any operating system. In addition, if research, you will notice that most of the sites run on Python such as YouTube and Google. Pyramid and Django are frameworks that support Python exclusively, same as the micro-framework like Flask and Bottle, which also supports Python. Python programming is mostly made up of English language keywords. You will master Python if you can learn the keywords. It will need some practice, and you need to familiarize yourself with the basic concepts before you begin. So, let's start by going through some of them:

Properties

Python is dynamically typed, and there is no need to state the variables. The variable is case sensitive; the types are enforced. For example, VAR and var are identified as two separate variables. To find out how any of the objects work, type the following command:

help(object)

Also, dir(object) to find all the methods of a certain option and use object.__doc__ to know the document string.

Data types

The next concept is data types. Lists, dictionaries, and tuples are data structures in Python. There are sets of libraries that are available in all versions of Python. Lists are the same as the one-dimensional array, and there can be lists of other different lists. The associative arrays, such as Dictionaries, while the one-dimensional arrays are the Tuples. Python arrays are any type, and it's always zero. A negative number starts from the end to the beginning.

Functions

The keyword 'def' is used to declare functions. Mandatory and optional arguments are simultaneously set in the function through assigning default values. An argument is assigned a value, and the functions can be returned to the tuple, which can effectively return values using the tuple unpacking. Connecting an object to a variable will remove an older one and also replace the immutable type. There is a lot of information on Python programming. As always, the main aim is to learn to program, mostly Python. Keep on experimenting and practicing programming to gain the skills and experience. It has a massive array of libraries and functions that you learn and taps into. There are great books and online resources to learn in-depth about Python programming, from error handling, subsets, and classes. You will encounter syntax errors galore, however, keep moving ahead, and you can join the fantastic Python communities and various resources, and you will master it in no time.

The Terms used in Python Programming

As it is the case for any skill, before going full-fledged into practicing the mode, it's important to learn the basic terms that are used in that domain. To better understand your domain, you should learn the terms. For a beginner in Python Programming, we bring a few essential terms that you can be your learning 101 guides. Below goes the programming terminology for beginners:

Algorithm

A set of rules that are created to solve an exact error. Tan error can be complex, such as converting video files to a different format, or simply, such as adding two numbers.

Program

This is an organized collection of instructions that performs a specific function when executed. It is processed by the CPU, an acronym for the central processing unit of the computer, before executed. Microsoft Word is an example of a program that enables users to create and edit documents. Also, the browsers used are programs that are created to help users to browse the internet.

API

API is an acronym for Application Programming Interfaces. Sets of rules and procedures for building software applications. The APIs help with communication with third party programs, which is used to build different software. Major companies like Facebook and Twitter frequently use APIs to assist the developers to easily gain access to their services.

Bytecode

Python combines the source code into bytecode, an internal presentation of the Python program in a CPython interpreter. Basically, the bytecode is an intermediate language running a virtual machine.

The virtual machine is converted into machine code for it to execute it; however, the one-byte cannot run on a different virtual machine.

Bug

A bud is a term used to refer to an unexpected error in hardware or software, which causes it not to function. Bugs are often regarded as small computer glitches; however, bugs are life-threatening conditions and causing substantial financial losses. That's why it is important to focus on the process of finding bugs before programs in the applications, and this process is called testing.

Code

This is a term used to describe a written set of rules that are written using protocols of different languages like Python or Java. And also an informal use of the code describing text that is written in a specific language, and the reference code can be made for different languages such as CCS Code or HTML Code.

Command-line interface

This is a user interface that is based on the text, and it is used in viewing and managing computer files. The interface is also referred to as the command-line user, character user, and console users. In the early 60s, 70s, and 80s, the primary means of interaction with computers on terminals was the command-line interface.

Compilation

Creating an executable program by writing the code in a compiled programming language is known as compilation. With compiling, the computer understands the program and runs it without using the programming software that was used to create it. The compiler translates the computer programs that were written using numbers and letters to a machine language program. C++ is an example of a compiler.

Constants

This is also referred to as Const is a term that describes a value that doesn't change through the execution of the program as opposed to a variable. Constant is fixed and cannot be changed; it can be a string, number, or character.

Data Types

This is a group of a particular type of data. A computer cannot differentiate between a name or a number as a human, so it uses a special internal code to know the difference in the types of data it receives and how to process it.

There are various data types, which include character, which is the alphabets, the boolean values are the TRUE or FALSE, the integer is the numbers, and the floating-point number is the decimal numbers.

Array

The array is a list of a grouped type of data values, and the values have the same data type; however, they are different by the positioning in the array.

For example, the age of students in a class is an array because they are all numbers, and also, the student's names in a class are array because of it's a character data type.

Declaration

This is a statement describing a variable, function, or other identifiers. It helps the compiler to identify the word, understand its meaning, and how to continue the process.

They are essential, however, optional and are useful depending on the type of programming language.

Exception

The unexpected and special condition that is encountered during the execution of a program. This is also an error or a condition that changes the program to a different path. For example, when a program loads a file from the disk but the file does not exist. In order to avoid any fatal error, it's highly important to handle and eradicate the exceptions in the program code.

Coroutine

A subroutine enters one point and exits in another point while a coroutine is generalized meaning; it enters, exits, and also resumes at many different points. A coroutine is implemented with the async def statement.

Generic Function

Multiple functions are implementing a similar operation for different types. A dispatch algorithm will decide on which implementation to be used during a call.

Python Expression

A piece of code that is evaluated to a value. It's a collection of expression elements such as function calls, names, operators, and literals. An if-statement is not an assignment or an expression because it doesn't return a value.

Python Decorator

A function that returns another function. It joins functionality without modifying it.

Loop

It is a series of instructions repeating a similar process that continues until a condition is completed, and it receives a command to stop. Then a question is asked on the program, and an answer will command the program to act, and then the loop continues to achieve a similar task. The process continues until there is no required action, and the code proceeds on. Loops are one of the most straightforward and powerful concepts in programming.

Chapter 2:

Getting ready for python

You can run and code Python on Windows, Mac, and Linux. To get started, head over to the official website: *www.python.org* and download the Python installer. This book will use Windows as the primary environment for examples and lessons.

Python 2.x vs. Python 3.x

There are two popular and official versions of Python: Python 3.x and 2.x. As of this writing, you can download Python 3.7.0 if you want the 3.x version. You can also download Python 2.7.15 if you want the 2.x version.

However, to prevent any conflicts and misunderstandings, please download and use Python 3.x. All the examples and lessons in this book are written with Python 3.x in mind.

The 2.x version is an older version of Python. Ever since the Python developers proceeded in developing Python 3.x, they have made a lot of changes to the behavior and even the syntax of the Python programming languages.

For example, if you divide 3 and 2 using the '/' operator in Python 2.x, you will receive an output of 1. If you divide the same numbers with the same operator in Python 3.x, you will receive an output of 1.5.

You may ask: If Python 3.x is new and improved, why are the developers keeping the old versions and why is Python 2.x being used? The quick answer to that is *code migration* because there are many differences between version 2.x and version 3.x, programs and scripts created using version 2.x need to be recoded to become compatible with version 3.x Python. If you are dealing with a small program using version 2.x, then the code migration will be a trivial problem at best. However, if you have programs with thousands of lines, then migration can become a huge problem. Other issues with migrating to Python 3.x are code maintenance and retraining programmers to adapt to the changes. Because of the aforementioned reasons, developers with huge programs written and ran using the version 2.x runtime environment did not bother making the transition to version 3.x.

Installing the Interpreter

Python comes with two important 'programs': Python's runtime environment and command-line interpreter. The Python installer you download from its website contains both. Installing them is easy, particularly in Windows. All you need to do is download the file and click open to let it run the setup. You will need to follow a few simple step-by-step instructions, click a few buttons here and there and Python will be available on your computer. Note that there will be a point during the installation that you will need to select the packages and features that you want to be installed in your system. Make sure that you check all of them. Note that tcl/tk installs TkInter, which is a Graphic User Interface (GUI) toolkit you need if you plan to create windows for your programs. The Integrated Development and Learning Environment (IDLE) require and depend on TkInter since it is a Python program with a GUI.

Also, for now, check the Python test suite feature. You will need it later. Finally, PIP is an optional feature that allows you to download Python packages later. If you believe you do not need some of them, just make sure that the checkbox for IDLE and Python Test Suite are selected.

Running Python

Python can be run on a system in three ways.

Interactive Interpreter

You can start by entering Python and then begin programming in its interpreter by beginning from the command line on any platform that provides a command line interpreter or a shell window.

A list of command line options is given in the table below.

Option	Description
-d	Provide the output after debugging
-O	Optimized byte code generation *i.e.*, the .pyo file is generated
-S	Don't run the import site for searching Python paths in a startup.
-v	Details of the import statement
-X	Disable the class-based built-in exceptions
-c cmd	It runs Python script sent in cmd String
File	The python script is run from the given file

Script from Command-line

Calling an interpreter on your application can help you run and execute your Python script in the command line.

Integrated Development Environment

It is possible to run Python from a GUI too. The one thing you require is a system that supports Python.

First Program

Once installed, you can quickly verify that everything is set by launching the terminal and typing "python" to launch the interpreter. Remember, Python is an interpreted language where each statement can be interpreted and executed without having to be compiled for each platform separately. An interpreter is an interactive tool that comes pre-bundled with all python installations, which can be used to quickly execute and verify python statements. The interpreter can be used to execute Python statements and see output immediately, without having to go through the hassle of creating a file and executing it to learn basic python statements. It is also a handy tool when one needs to experiment to correct errors in programming and debug. Let us now write our infamous "Hello World "program and officially get started with writing programs in Python.

>python

>>>>>>print "Hello World"

Hello World

One statement is all it takes - no fancy imports or function blocks required. The keyword "print," is sufficient to instruct the interpreter to print anything that is enclosed within " ".

Since it is an interpreter-driven language, the same interactive interpreter can double up and be used as a calculator; for example, you can perform basic math operations as follows:

>python

>>>>>>3+5

>>>>>>8

>>>>>>5-2

>>>>>>3

And so forth. Just play around by executing various python statements directly from the interpreter and check the output to learn the basics. You can exit from the interpreter at any time by using one of the following commands,

>>> ctrl + d

Or

>>>exit()

Or

>>>quit()

With Python installed, and after having tested our first piece of code with the programming language, we are all set to delve deeper and explore the magical world of python programming! Let us get rolling!

Basic Program Structure

Now, let us learn some more about the basics of writing longer python code. So far, what we have seen are simple python statements, with many of these cohesive statements forming a code block and many such blocks making up the whole program. Therefore, for more serious programming, it becomes imperative to use a text editor and have the statements bundled together into files. Let us now look at how to create a simple python program and execute it from a file. The official IDE for python is IDEAL; however, you can use any editor of your choice, like vim, sublime text, notepad, *etc.* Open a new file and type in the succeeding statement:

print "Hello World"

Now, save the file with the name of your choice, with as.py as the extension, like HelloWorld.py in our case, and you have officially created your first program file with Python. Now, launch the terminal, navigate to the file path and execute the python script using the following command to execute the file, and watch the program run.

>python./HelloWorld.py

This command basically launches the interpreter and instructs it to take the file named "HelloWorld.py" from the current directory (./) and execute the statements.

>Hello World

The output is now delivered onto the console, so in our case, the string "Hello World" is printed. The file can also be executed by simply typing./HelloWorld.py on the terminal after launching the interpreter. The python program file can also be executed as follows:

>>> execfile("helloworld.py")

Hello World

The execfile() API will look for the file in the mentioned path, which in our case is the current directory and then run the script.

White Spaces and Indentation

The python statements do not have an end of line delimiters such as the ";" used in languages like C or C++. When typing the statement "print "Hello World", it does not require a ";" to mark its end. This also means that the blocks/statements of a python program are marked by means of spaces and indentation.

Therefore, in any given Python program, white spaces and indentation are extremely important components, and if used incorrectly, could cause errors.

Unlike other languages, white spaces are extremely important in python programming, and if used incorrectly, they could cause some serious errors preventing the execution of the program itself.

White spaces in the beginning mark different blocks of the program. Blocks are differentiated from one another based on indentation, with space before a statement denoting the beginning of a new block, and indent to end the block. In addition, each letter or word is separated using white spaces.

```
>>>>a = 5
```

```
>>>> a = 5
```

```
^ a= 5
```

Unexpected indentation error

The first statement compiles fine (we will learn more about what this statement does in the next chapter), but the second statement will give you an error due to the inappropriately placed extra space at the beginning of the second statement, before the "a". With spaces being so important, as a rule of thumb, the following basic rules should be followed with respect to white lines and indentation to have a uniformly understood code,

Use 4 spaces to denote indentation

Do not mix spaces and tab

Always leave one-line spacing between two functions

To separate two classes, use two-line spacing

Comment statements begin with # and are a single line,

#This comment is a single line.

To have multi-line comments in a python file, enclose the statements using triple quotes as follows,

'''

This comment is a multi-line statement for python

'''

Let us now look at a couple more examples using the rules regarding white space and comments that we have learned. Save the following bunch of lines in a .py file and execute them at once, or you can execute them one by one using the interpreter.

print "This is a sample program"

print 3+4 #this prints the sum of the two numbers

#print 3+4 #this statement is itself a comment hence nothing happens.

With the basic rules set, let us now delve deeper and uncover the powerful data types that python offers and how we can use them to write elegant and powerful code.

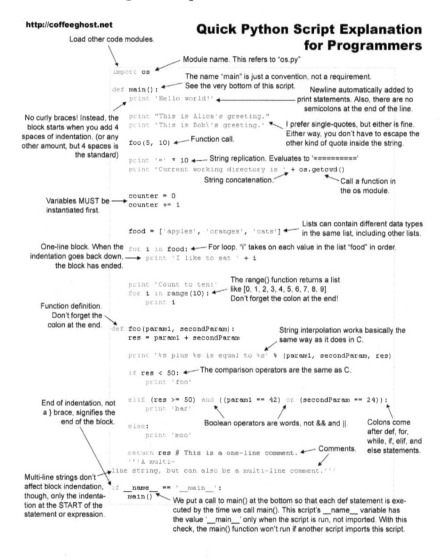

Chapter 3:

Learning the basics of python programming

The Basics of the Python Language

Now that we know a bit more about the Python language and some of the things that we are able to do in order to see results with this kind of language, it is time to learn a few of the different basic parts that are needed in this kind of coding language before you even write out a single code with it at all. There are a lot of different parts that come into play, so let's dive right in and get started.

Python Keywords

The first thing that we need to take a look at in this section is the Python keywords. Just like with other languages that we may work with, we will find that these are reserved words that we are able to use to provide a command to our compiler.

You should make sure that they are only used in the proper place in your code and that you are not bringing them up randomly, or you will end up with an error in the code that you are writing.

These are reserved because they are meant to provide your compiler with the instructions that it needs in order to handle your coding at that time.

These keywords are already programmed into the compiler to make sure that it behaves well. Because of this, you will find that they are going to be important to any kind of code that you are trying to write. Make sure that you learn what these works are all about and how they are going to work with the compiler so that you can be on the lookout.

Naming Our Identifiers

The first rule to remember is when you name these identifiers. You have many options when you are naming your identifiers. For example, you can rely on both uppercase and lowercase letters with naming, as well as any number and the underscore symbol. You can also combine any of these together. One thing to remember here is that you can't start the name with a number, and there shouldn't be any spaces between the words that you write out. So, you can't write out "3words" as a name, but you can write out "words3" or three words. Make sure that you don't use one of the keywords that we discussed above, or you will end up with an error.

Control Flow Basics

In many languages, the control flow that comes with it is going to be an important thing as well. The control flow that comes with Python is going to be pretty important as well because it helps us to know whether or not we are correctly writing the code. There are going to be a few strings that we need to pay careful attention to because they need to be read by the compiler properly.

If you are not using the control flow in the right manner, then you will end up with the compiler being confused and then you will get some error messages. The good news here is that we are going to spend some time looking at a lot of examples of codes in this guidebook, and you will be able to figure out what is right and what is wrong with the control flow that you are working with.

Python Comments

The next thing that we need to spend some time on is the comments. As you are working with some of the codes that you would like to write, you may find that there are some situations where you would like to add in a little note or some other explanation on what is being written inside of that particular code. And you want to be able to do this without causing the compiler to get confused or making it impossible to finish up the code without an error.

These are little notes that can be important to others who are using or reading through the code, but we do not want them to show up in the code when it is executed. And this is going to be known as a comment in the Python language, as well as with some of the other coding languages that you want to work with. Any comment that you write out with Python will be ignored and passed over by the compiler, as long as you use the # symbol ahead of what you are writing. This symbol is going to tell the compiler that you are writing out a comment and that it should avoid reading that comment and instead move on to another part of the code to handle. With the Python language, you technically are able to add in as many of these comments as you would like to help explain to yourself or others what you have written at that part of the code. If you would like to have one on every other line of the code, then this is technically allowed. Keep in mind, though, that this is going to make your code look a bit messy and unprofessional, so it is generally something that is avoided. Just add in the number of comments that are needed and don't go overboard, and your code will work great. We will talk about the next two topics a bit more in some of the following chapters because they are so important to what we are going to be doing throughout our coding experience, but they still deserve a bit of mention here.

We are going to take some time to look at two more important topics that are the basis of your Python code, whether these codes are simple or more complex, including the operators and variables.

Variables

Variables are another part of the code that you will need to know about because they are so common in your code. The variables are there to help store some of the values that you place in the code, helping them to stay organized and nice. You can easily add in some of the values to the right variable simply by using the equal sign. It is even possible for you to take two values and add them to the same variables if you want, and you will see this occur in a few of the codes that we discuss through this guidebook. Variables are very common, and you will easily see them throughout the examples that we show.

Operators

Then we are able to move on to some of the operators that you will be able to use. While you are coding, you will quickly notice that these operators are all over the place. And there are quite a few of them that you are able to handle along the way as well. Learning how to work with these operators can make code writing a little bit easier and will help us to make sure that our codes will work the way that we want. These are just a few of the different parts of working with the Python code that we are able to focus on. These parts are going to be critical to ensuring that we are not going to lose out on some of the work that we need to handle and can make it easier for us to understand some of the more complex codes that we will focus on at a later time. Make sure to review these parts and gain a good understanding of how they work to help make it a bit easier when it is time to work with the codes that are coming up.

Chapter 4:

The world of operators and variables

The Python Variables

The Python variables are an important thing to work with as well. A variable, in simple terms, is often just going to be a box that we can use to hold onto the values and other things that show up in our code. They will reserve a little bit of the memory of our code so that we are able to utilize it later. These are important because they allow us to pull out the values that we would like to use at a later time without issues along the way.

These variables will be a good topic to discuss because they will be stored inside the memory of our code. And you will then be able to assign a value over to them and pull them out in the code that you would like to use. These values are going to be stored in some part of the memory of your code and will be ready to use when you need. Depending on the type of data that you will work with, the variable is going to be the part that can tell your compiler the right place to save that information to pull it out easier.

With this in mind, the first thing that we need to take a look at is how to assign a value over to the variable. To get the variable to behave in the manner that you would like, you need to make sure that a minimum of one value is assigned to it. Otherwise, you are just saving an empty spot in the memory. If the variable is assigned properly to some value, and sometimes more than one value based on the code you are using, then it is going to behave in the proper manner, and when you call up that variable, the right value will show up. As you go through and work with some of the variables you have, you may find that there are three main options that are able to use. Each of these can be useful, and it is often going to depend on what kind of code you would like to create on the value that you want to put with a particular variable. The three main types of variable that you are able to choose from here will include:

Float

This would include numbers like 3.14 and so on.

String

This will be like a statement where you could write out something like "Thank you for visiting my page!" or another similar phrase.

Whole number

This would be any of the other numbers that you would use that do not have a decimal point.

When you are working with variables in your code, you need to remember that you don't need to take the time to make a declaration to save up this spot in the memory. This is automatically going to happen once you assign a value over to the variable using the equal sign. If you want to check that this is going to happen, just look to see that you added that equal sign in, and everything is going to work.

Assigning a value over to your variable is pretty easy. Some examples of how you can do this in your code would include the following:

x = 12 #this is an example of an integer assignment

pi = 3.14 #this is an example of a floating-point assignment

customer name = John Doe #this is an example of a string assignment

There is another option that we are able to work with on this one, and one that we have brought up a few times within this section already. This is where we will assign more than one value to one for our variables. There are a few cases where we will write out our code, and then we need to make sure that there are two or more values that go with the same variable.

To make this happen, you just need to use the same kind of procedure that we were talking about before. Of course, we need to make sure that each part is attached to the variable with an equal sign. This helps the compiler know ahead of time that these values are all going to be associated with the same variable. So, you would write out something like a = b= c= 1 to show the compiler that all of the variables are going to equal one. Or you could do something like 1 = b = 2 in order to show that there are, in this case, two values that go with one variable.

The thing that you will want to remember when you are working with these variables is that you have to assign a value in order to make the work happen in the code. These variables are also just going to be spots in your code that are going to reserve some memory for the values of your choice.

The Python Operators

The Python operators are going to be pretty diverse and can do a lot of different things in your code based on how you use them. When we are talking about the operators, there are going to be quite a few different types that you are able to work with in the code. Let's explore a bit more about these operators and how we are able to use these for our needs as well.

Arithmetic Operators

The first type of operator that we are going to take a look at is the arithmetic operators. These are going to be similar to the signals and signs that we would use when we do mathematical equations. You can work with the addition, subtraction, multiplication, and division symbols in order to do the same kinds of actions on the different parts of the code that you are working with. These are common when you want to do something like add two parts of the code together with one another. You have the freedom to add in as many of these to your code as you would like, and you can even put more than one type in the same statement. Just remember that you need to work with the rules of operation and do these in the right order in order to make it work the way that you would like. Otherwise, you will be able to add in as many of these to the same code as you need to make it work.

Operator	Description	Exam
+	Adds two operands	A + B
-	Subtracts second operand from the first	A - B
*	Multiply both operands	A * B
/	Divide numerator by denumerator	B / A
%	Modulus Operator and remainder of after an integer division	B % A
++	Increment operator, increases integer value by one	A++
--	Decrement operator, decreases integer value by one	A-- w

The above is going to be some of the different operators that you are able to work with that fit into this category.

Working with these will ensure that we are able to handle the work and that we will be able to use inside of our codes.

Comparison Operators

After looking at the arithmetic operators, it is also possible for us to work with the comparison operators. These comparison operators are going to be good to work with because they will let you take over two, and sometimes more, values and statements in the code and then see how they are going to compare to one another.

This is one that we will often use for a lot of codes that are going to rely on Boolean expressions because it ensures that the answer you get back with be false and true. So your statements in this situation are going to be the same as each other, or they will be different.

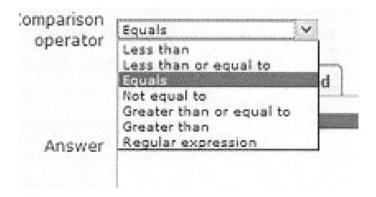

There are a lot of times when we will be able to work with these comparison operators to get the most out of the programming that we are doing.

You need to consider these ahead of time and make sure that we will be able to get the results that we need in our code.

Logical Operators

Next, we are going to be looking at the logical operators. These may not be used as often as the other options, but it is still some time for us to look it over.

These operators are going to be used when it is time to evaluate the input that a user is able to present to us, with any of the conditions that you are able to set in your code.

There are going to be three types of logical operators that we are able to work with, and some of the examples that you are going to use in order to work with this in your code include:

Not

If ends up being false, the compiler is going to return True. But if x ends up being true, the program will return false.

A	B	A AND B	A OR B	NO
False	False	False	False	True
False	True	False	True	True
True	False	False	True	Fals
True	True	True	True	Fals

The chart above is going to show us a bit more about the logical operators that we are able to work with as well. This can give us a good idea of what is going to happen when we use each of the operators for our own needs as well.

Assignment Operators

And the final type of operator that we are going to take a look at is the assignment operator. This is going to be the kind of operator that will show up, and if you take a look at some of the different codes that we have already taken a look at in this guidebook, you will be able to see them quite a bit. This is because the assignment operator is simply going to be an equal sign, where you will assign a value over to a variable throughout the code.

So, if you are looking to assign the number 100 over to one of your variables, you would just need to put the equal sign there between them. This can be used with any kind of variable and value that you are using in your code, and you should already have some familiarity with getting this done ahead of time. It is also possible for you to go through and take several values, assigning them to the same variable if that is best for your code. As long as you have this assignment operator, or the equal sign, in between it, you will be able to add in as many values over to the variable that you would like.

Working with these operators is a simple thing to work with, but you will find that they show up in your coding on a regular basis. You are able to use them to add your variables together, to use other mathematical operators, to assign a value over to the variable, or even a few values to your same variable. And you are able to even take these operators to compare two or more parts of the code at the same time and see I they are the same or not. As we can already see, there are so many things that we will be able to do when it comes to using these operators.

Chapter 5:

Python Data types

Numbers

As mentioned earlier, Python accommodates floating, integer, and complex numbers. The presence or absence of a decimal point separates integers and floating points. For instance, 4 is an integer, while 4.0 is a floating-point number. On the other hand, complex numbers in Python are denoted as r+tj, where j represents the real part, and t is the virtual part. In this context, the function type() is used to determine the variable class. The Python function is instance() is invoked to make a determination of which specific class function originates from.

Example:

Start IDLE.

Navigate to the File menu and click New Window.

Type the following:

number=6

 print(type(number)) #should output class int print(type(6.0)) #should output class float complex_num=7+5j

print(complex_num+5)

print(isinstance(complex_num, complex)) #should output True

Important: Integers in Python can be of infinite length. Floating numbers in Python are assumed precise up to fifteen decimal places.

Number Conversion

This segment assumes you have prior basic knowledge of how to manually or using a calculator to convert decimal into binary, octal, and hexadecimal. Check out the Windows Calculator in Windows 10, Calculator version 10.1804.911.1000, and choose programmer mode to automatically convert.

Programmers often need to convert decimal numbers into octal, hexadecimal, and binary forms. A prefix in Python allows denotation of these numbers to their corresponding type.

Number System Prefix

Octal '0O' or '0o'

Binary '0B' or '0b'

Hexadecimal '0X or '0x'

Example

print(0b1010101) #Output:85

print(0x7B+0b0101) #Output: 128 (123+5) print(0o710) #Output:710

Assignment

Create a program in Python to display the following: i) 0011 11112

ii) 7478

iii) 9316

Type Conversion

Sometimes referred to as coercion, type conversion allows us to change one type of number into another. The preloaded functions such as float(), int(), and complex() enable implicit and explicit type conversions. The same functions can be used to change from strings.

Example

Start IDLE.

Navigate to the File menu and click New Window.

Type the following:

int(5.3) #Gives 5

int(5.9) #Gives 5

The int() will produce a truncation effect when applied to floating numbers. It will simply drop the decimal point part without rounding off.

For the float() let us take a look: Start IDLE. Navigate to the File menu and click New Window.

Type the following:

float(6) #Gives 6.0

ccomplex('4+2j') #Gives (4+2j)

Assignment

Apply the int() conversion to the following: a. 4.1

b. 4.7

c. 13.3

d. 13.9

Apply the float() conversion to the following: e. 7

f. 16

g. 19

Decimal in Python

Example

Start IDLE.

Navigate to the File menu and click New Window.

Type the following:

```
(1.2+2.1)==3.3 #Will return False, why?
```

Explanation

The computer works with finite numbers and fractions cannot be stored in their raw form as they will create infinite long binary sequence.

Fractions in Python

The fractions module in Python allows operations on fractional numbers.

Example

Start IDLE.

Navigate to the File menu and click New Window.

Type the following:

Important

Creating my_fraction from float can lead to unusual results due to the misleading representation of binary floating point.

Mathematics in Python

To carry out mathematical functions, Python offers modules like random and math.

Start IDLE.

Navigate to the File menu and click New Window.

Type the following:

import math

print(math.pi) #output:3.14159....

print(math.cos(math.pi)) #the output will be -1.0

print(math.exp(10)) #the output will be 22026.4....

print(math.log10(100)) #the output will be 2

print(math.factorial(5)) #the output will be 120

Exercise

Write a python program that uses math functions from the math module to perform the following: a. Square of 34

b. Log1010000

c. Cos 45 x sin 90

d. Exponent of 20

Random function in Python

Start IDLE.

Navigate to the File menu and click New Window.

Type the following:

```
import math
print(random.shuffle_num(11, 21)) y=['f','g','h','m']
print(random.pick(y))
random.anypic(y)
print(y)
print(your_pick.random())
```

Lists in Python

We create a list in Python by placing items called elements inside square brackets separated by commas. The items in a list can be of mixed data type.

Start IDLE.

Navigate to the File menu and click New Window.

Type the following:

```
list_mine=[] #empty list list_mine=[2,5,8] #list of integers
list_mine=[5,"Happy", 5.2] #list having mixed data types
```

Assignment

Write a program that captures the following in a list: "Best", 26,89,3.9

Nested Lists

A nested list is a list as an item in another list.

Example

Start IDLE.

Navigate to the File menu and click New Window.

Type the following:

list_mine=["carrot", [9, 3, 6], ['g']]

Exercise

Write a nested for the following elements: [36,2,1],"Writer",'t',[3.0, 2.5]

Accessing Elements from a List

In programming and in Python specifically, the first time is always indexed zero. For a list of five items we will access them from index0 to index4. Failure to access the items in a list in this manner will create index error. The index is always an integer as using other number types will create a type error. For nested lists, they are accessed via nested indexing.

Example

Start IDLE.

Navigate to the File menu and click New Window.

Type the following:

list_mine=['b','e','s','t']

print(list_mine[0]) #the output will be b print(list_mine[2]) #the output will be s print(list_mine[3]) #the output will be t
Exercise

Given the following list:

your_collection=['t','k','v','w','z','n','f']

a. Create a program in Python to display the second item in the list b. Create a program in Python to display the sixth item in the last c. Create a program in Python to display the last item in the list.

Nested List Indexing

Start IDLE.

Navigate to the File menu and click New Window.

Type the following:

nested_list=["Best',[4,7,2,9]]

print(nested_list[0][1]

Python Negative Indexing

For its sequences, Python allows negative indexing. The last item on the list is index-1, index -2 is the second last item and so on.

Start IDLE.

Navigate to the File menu and click New Window.

Type the following:

list_mine=['c','h','a','n','g','e','s']

print(list_mine[-1]) #Output is s print(list_mine [-4]) ##Output is n Slicing Lists in Python

Slicing operator(full colon) is used to access a range of elements in a list.

Example

Start IDLE.Navigate to the File menu and click New Window.

Type the following:

```
list_mine=['c','h','a','n','g','e','s']
print(list_mine[3:5]) #Picking elements from the 4 to the sixth
```

Example

Picking elements from start to the fifth Start IDLE.

Navigate to the File menu and click New Window.

Type the following:

```
print(list_mine[:-6])
```

Example

Picking the third element to the last.

```
print(list_mine[2:])
```

Exercise

Given class_names=['John', 'Kelly', 'Yvonne', 'Una','Lovy','Pius', 'Tracy']

a. Write a python program using slice operator to display from the second students and the rest.

b. Write a python program using slice operator to display first student to the third using negative indexing feature.

c. Write a python program using slice operator to display the fourth and fifth students only.

Manipulating Elements in a List using the assignment operator

Items in a list can be changed meaning lists are mutable.

Start IDLE.

Navigate to the File menu and click New Window.

Type the following:

list_yours=[4,8,5,2,1]

list_yours[1]=6

print(list_yours) #The output will be [4,6,5,2,1

Changing a range of items in a list

Start IDLE.

Navigate to the File menu and click New Window.

Type the following:

list_yours[0:3]=[12,11,10] #Will change first item to fourth item in the list print(list_yours) #Output will be: [12,11,10,1]

Appending/Extending items in the List

The append() method allows extending the items in the list. The extend() can also be used.

Example

Start IDLE.

Navigate to the File menu and click New Window.

Type the following:

list_yours=[4, 6, 5]

list_yours.append(3)

print(list_yours) #The output will be [4,6,5, 3]

Example

Start IDLE.

Navigate to the File menu and click New Window.

Type the following:

list_yours=[4,6,5]

list_yours.extend([13,7,9]) print(list_yours) #The output will be [4,6,5,13,7,9]

The plus operator(+) can also be used to combine two lists. The * operator can be used to perform iteration of a list a given severally.

Example

Start IDLE.

Navigate to the File menu and click New Window.

Type the following:

list_yours=[4,6,5]

print(list_yours+[13,7,9]) # Output:[4, 6, 5,13,7,9]

print(['happy']*4)   #Output:["happy","happy", "happy","happy"]

Removing or Deleting Items from a List

The keyword del is used to delete elements or the entire list in Python.

Example

Start IDLE.

Navigate to the File menu and click New Window.

Type the following:

list_mine=['t','r','o','g','r','a','m']

del list_mine[1]

print(list_mine) #t, o, g, r, a, m

Deleting Multiple Elements

Example

Start IDLE.

Navigate to the File menu and click New Window.

Type the following:

del list_mine[0:3]

Example

print(list_mine) #a, m

Delete Entire List

Start IDLE.

Navigate to the File menu and click New Window.

Type the following:

delete list_mine

print(list_mine) #will generate an error of lost not found The remove() method or pop() function may be used to remove the specified item. The pop() method will remove and return the last item if the index is not given and helps implement lists as stacks. The clear() method is used to empty a list.

Start IDLE.

Navigate to the File menu and click New Window.

Type the following:

list_mine=['t','k','b','d','w','q','v']

list_mine.remove('t')

print(list_mine) #output will be ['t','k','b','d','w','q','v']

print(list_mine.pop(1)) #output will be 'k'

print(list_mine.pop()) #output will be 'v'

Assignment

Given list_yours=['K','N','O','C','K','E','D']

a. Pop the third item in the list, save the program as list1.

b. Remove the fourth item using remove() method and save the program as list2

c. Delete the second item in the list and save the program as list3.

d. Pop the list without specifying an index and save the program as list4.

Using Empty List to Delete an entire or specific elements

Start IDLE.

Navigate to the File menu and click New Window.

Type the following:

list_mine=['t','k','b','d','w','q','v']

list_mine=[1:2]=[]

print(list_mine) #Output will be ['t','w','q','v']

 List Methods in Python

Assignment

Use list access methods to display the following items in reversed order list_yours=[4,9,2,1,6,7]

Use list access method to count the elements in a.

Use list access method to sort the items in a. in an ascending order/default.

 Inbuilt Python Functions that can be used to manipulate Python Lists

 Tuple in Python

A tuple is like a list but we cannot change elements in a tuple.

Example

Start IDLE.

Navigate to the File menu and click New Window.

Type the following:

tuple_mine = (21, 12, 31)

print(tuple_mine)

tuple_mine = (31, "Green", 4.7) print(tuple_mine)

Accessing Python Tuple Elements

Example

Start IDLE.

Navigate to the File menu and click New Window.

Type the following:

tuple_mine=['t','r','o','g','r','a','m']

print(tuple_mine[1]) #output:'r'

print(tuple_mine[3]) #output:'g'

Negative Indexing

Just like lists, tuples can also be indexed negatively.

Like lists, -1 refers to the last element on the list and -2 refer to the second last element.

Example

Start IDLE.

Navigate to the File menu and click New Window.

Type the following:

tuple_mine=['t','r','o','g','r','a','m']

print(tuple_mine [-2]) #the output will be 'a'

Slicing

The slicing operator, the full colon is used to access a range of items in a tuple.

Example

Start IDLE.

Navigate to the File menu and click New Window.

Type the following:

tuple_mine=['t','r','o','g','r','a','m']

print(tuple_mine [2:5]) #Output: 'o','g','r','a'

print(tuple_mine[:-4]) #'g','r','a','m'

Note

Tuple elements are immutable, meaning they cannot be changed. However, we can combine elements in a tuple using +(concatenation operator). We can also repeat elements in a tuple using the * operator, just like lists.

Example

Start IDLE.

Navigate to the File menu and click New Window.

Type the following:

print((7, 45, 13) + (17, 25, 76)) print(("Several",) * 4) *Note*

Since we cannot change elements in tuple, we cannot delete the elements too.

However, removing the full tuple can be attained using the keyword del. Example

Start IDLE.

Navigate to the File menu and click New Window.

Type the following:

t_mine=['t','k','q','v','y','c','d']

del t_mine

Available Tuple Methods in Python

They are only two methods available for working Python tuples.

count(y)

When called will give the item numbers that are equal to y.

index(y)

When called will give index first item index that is equal to y.

Example

Start IDLE.

Navigate to the File menu and click New Window.

Type the following:

t_mine=['t','k','q','v','y','c','d']

print(t_mine.count('t'))

print(t_mine.index('l'))

Testing Membership in Tuple

The keyword in us used to check the specified element exists in a tuple.

Start IDLE.

Navigate to the File menu and click New Window.

Type the following:

t_mine=['t','k','q','v','y','c','d']

print('a' t_mine) #Output: True print('k' in t_mine) #Output: False

Inbuilt Python Functions with Tuple

String in Python

Example

Start IDLE.

Navigate to the File menu and click New Window.

Type the following:

string_mine = 'Colorful'

print(string_mine)

string_mine = "Hello"

print(string_mine)

string_mine = '''Hello'''

print(string_mine)

string_mine = """I feel like I have been born a programmer"""

print(string_mine)

Accessing items in a string

Example

Start IDLE.

Navigate to the File menu and click New Window.

Type the following:

```
str = 'Colorful'

print('str = ', str)

print('str[1] = ', str[1]) #Output the second item print('str[-2] = ', str[-2]) #Output the second last item print('str[2:4] = ', str[2:4]) #Output the third through the fifth item
```

Deleting or Changing in Python

In Python, strings are immutable therefore cannot be changed once assigned.

However, deleting the entire string is possible.

Example

Start IDLE.

Navigate to the File menu and click New Window.

Type the following:

```
del string_mine
```

String Operations

Several operations can be performed on a string, making it a widely used data type in Python.

Concatenation using the + operator, repetition using the * operator Example

Start IDLE.

Navigate to the File menu and click New Window.

Type the following:

string1='Welcome'

string2='Again'

print('string1+string2=',string1+string2) print(' string1 * 3 =', string1 * 3) Exercise

Given string_a="I am awake" and string_b="coding in Python in a pajama"

String Iteration

The control statement is used to continually scan through an entire scan until the specified severally are reached before terminating the scan.

Example

Start IDLE. Navigate to the File menu and click New Window.

Type the following:

Membership Test in String

The keyword in is used to test if a sub string exists.

Example

't' in "triumph' #Will return True Inbuilt Python Functions for working with Strings They include enumerate() and len(). The len() function returns the length of the string.

String Formatting in Python

Escape Sequences

Single and Double Quotes

Example

Start IDLE.

Navigate to the File menu and click New Window.

Type the following:

```
print('They said, "We need a new team?"') # escape with single
quotes # escaping double quotes

print("They said, \" We need a new team\"")
```

Escape Sequences in Python

The escape sequences enable us to format our output to enhance clarity to the human user. A program will still run successfully without using escape sequences, but the output will be highly confusing to the human user. Writing and displaying output in expected output is part of good programming practices.

The following are commonly used escape sequences.

Examples

Start IDLE.

Navigate to the File menu and click New Window.

Type the following:

```
print("D:\\Lessons\\Programming") print("Prints\n in two
lines")
```

Chapter 6:

Building functions

Functions and Modules

Functions are code blocks that are given an identifier. This identifier can be used to call the function. Calling a function makes the program execute the function regardless of where it is located within the code. To create a function, you need to use the "def" keyword. Def basically defines, and when you use it to create a function, you can call it as defining a function. For example:

```
>>> def doSomething():
```

```
print("Hello functioning world!")
```

```
>>> doSomething()
```

Hello functioning world!

```
>>> _
```

Creating and calling a function is easy.

The primary purpose of a function is to allow you to organize, simplify, and modularize your code.

Whenever you have a set of code that you will need to execute in sequence from time to time, defining a function for that set of code will save you time and space in your program. Instead of repeatedly typing code or even copy-pasting, you simply define a function.

Arguments and Parameters

Aside from serving as a quick way to execute a block of code, functions can accept arguments through its parameters. What are the arguments and parameters anyway? Before I offer any explain, look at the below example: >>> def saySomething(thisIsaParameter):

```
 print(thisIsaParameter)
```

>>> saySomething("This Is An Argument")

This Is An Argument

>>> _

Think of it this way: parameters are questions, and arguments are answers. The keyword print has the parameter that requires you to input a string as an argument. Whenever you use the keyword print, it is asking you, "What do you want me to print?" You then reply with the string that you want the print keyword to display on the screen. In technical terms, parameters are private variables of functions. Whenever you call a function and indicate an argument for the parameter, you are basically assigning a value to the parameter, which the function can use as a regular variable. Note the word **private**. Since parameters are functions' private variables, no other function(s) can use them. Also, variables declared and used for the first time in a function will also be unavailable to others. Outside the scope of a function, all of its parameters and private variables are erased. This means that you cannot access their assigned value once the function has **completed** execution. For example: >>> def sampFunc(x):

```
 print(x)
```

>>> sampFunc("Sample String")

Sample String

```
>>> x
```

Traceback (most recent call last):

 File "<stdin>", line 1, in <module>

NameError: name 'x' is not defined

```
>>> _
```

By the way, the parentheses are important. They separate your parameters and arguments from your function's identifier or name. When calling a function, you always need to place those parentheses even if you have not set a parameter.

More about private variables and related topics will be discussed later.

Parameters Require Arguments

You cannot call a function with parameters without an argument. If you do, you will receive an error. For example:

```
>>> def sampFunc(x):
```

 print(x)

```
>>> sampFunc()
```

Traceback (most recent call last):

 File "<stdin>", line 1, in <module>

TypeError: y() missing 1 required positional argument: 'x'

```
>>> _
```

Multiple Parameters

You can assign two or more parameters in a function. For example:

>>> def simpOp(x, y):

z = x + y

 print(z)

>>> simpOp(1, 2)

3

>>> _

Passing Arguments by Value, Reference, and Assignment

In most programming languages, passing an argument using variables to a parameter can be done in two ways: value and reference.

If you pass an argument by value, the function will only take the value of the variable and assign it to the parameter. Here is an example using Visual Basic 6: Function f(ByVal a as Integer, ByVal b as Integer)

 a = a + b

<u>End Function</u>

Sub main()

 x = 1

 y = 2

 Call f(x + y)

End Sub

Variables x and y will still hold the value 1 and 2 respectively after calling the function f.

If you pass an argument by reference, the function will assign the parameter the variable itself. Any changes or manipulation on the parameter will reflect on the variable assigned.

Here is an example using Visual Basic 6:

Function f(ByRef a as Integer, ByRef b as Integer)

a = a + b

End Function

Sub main()

x = 1

y = 2

Call f(x + y)

End Sub

Variable y will still hold the value 2 while variable x will have the value 3 after calling the function f. Python works differently. Instead of passing variables as values and references, they are passed by assignment. It means that Python will pass the variable by value or reference depending on the type of data the variable contains. For example:

```
>>> x = 10
>>> def increment(y):
y += 1
```

```
>>> increment(x)

>>> x

10

>>> _
```

Python will pass by value if the variable contains an immutable object like a string. Python will pass by reference if the variable contains a mutable object like a list.

```
>>> x = [1, 2, 3, 4]

>>> def addItem(y):

y += [5, 6, 7, 8]

>>> addItem(x)

>>> x

[1, 2, 3, 4, 5, 6, 7, 8]

>>> _
```

Passing by reference seems convenient, especially if you need to manipulate data in a variable fast.

However, if you have strings and numbers, you are stuck with passing by value. For example: >>> x = 10

```
>>> y = 3

>>> def exponent(a, b):

a = a**b

print(a)
```

```
>>> exponent(x, y)
```

1000

```
>>> _
```

However, you want the value to be assigned to x instead of just printing it. You might try to solve this kind of problem by assigning the value to variable x directly inside the function like this: >>> x = 10

```
>>> y = 3
```

```
>>> def exponent(a, b):
```

```
x = a**b
```

```
print(x)
```

```
>>> exponent(x, y)
```

1000

```
>>> x
```

10

```
>>> _
```

Unfortunately, that will not work since Python will treat the variable x inside the function as one of the function's **private** variable.

Despite having the same name as the variable x outside the scope of the function, the variable x inside the function is different from it. One way to mitigate this kind of problem is to use the keyword **global**.

Note that variables outside the scope of functions are considered global variables. However, Global variables can be used inside functions, but you need to tell Python that it is a global variable by using the keyword **global**. Here is an example: >>> x = 10

>>> y = 3

>>> def exponent(a, b):

global x

x = a**b

print(x)

>>> exponent(x, y)

1000

>>> x

1000

>>> _

It seems that it solved the problem of not having a pass by reference for numbers. However, this is bad coding. Yes, you can do it, but it does not always mean that if you can do something, it is good.

First of all, most developers discourage the use of global variable. This is a debatable topic.

Second, this way of assigning value to a variable from a function is weak. What if you have a different variable and want to do the same to it. This piece of code will not do since it only changes variable x. It is true there is a workaround by making x as a temporary variable to hold the value of the function. For example: >>> x = 10

>>> y = 3

>>> z = 0

>>> def exponent(a, b):

global z

z = a**b

print(z)

>>> exponent(x, y)

1000

>>> x

10

>>> z

1000

>>> x = z

>>> x

1000

>>> _

It works, but you are still using a global variable and it makes your code messy. Yes, that is messy by default standards. The third reason why the previous example is a bad/inefficient code is that there is a better way to do it. And that is, by using the **return** keyword.

Returning Value

The return keyword makes a function return a value. For a simpler explanation, it makes the function be used as a variable that has an assigned or processed value.

For example: >>> def concat(string1, string2):

 return string1 + string2

>>> x = concat("Text1", "Text2")

>>> x

'Text1Text2'

>>> _

A function can return a value even if it does not have parameters. For example:

>>> def piString():

 return "3.14159265359"

>>> x = piString()

>>> x

'3.14159265359'

>>> _

As you can see, using the keyword method makes it simpler for you to retrieve a value from a function without relying on global variables.

Return allows you to make clean and efficient code.

Mutable and Immutable Objects

Now that you know the return statement, you can now work on passing arguments by reference and by value without worrying about the variable's mutability. By the way, mutability is a characteristic of an object that refers to its ability to mutate.

Whenever you process and **change** data, you mutate it. Put simply: a mutable object can be changed, and an immutable object cannot be changed. Immutable objects are integers, float, Boolean, string, and tuples. You can easily understand why tuples are immutable because they are lists that cannot be changed. However, you might get confused about why numbers, strings, and Boolean values are immutable. After all, you can change or reassign the number assigned to variable x anytime.

The keywords there are change and reassign. For example:

```
>>> x = 1

>>> x

1

>>> x = 2

>>> x

2

>>> _
```

Remember that everything in Python is an object. This includes numbers, strings, Boolean values, and etcetera. In the above example, 1 and 2 are two separate objects. Instead of mutating the object 1 assigned to variable x, you just **replace** it with object 2.

Here is another example:

```
>>> x = 1
>>> x
1
>>> x += 5
>>> x
6
>>> _
```

Python thinks of this as adding object 1 and object 5, and change the value of variable x to object 6. The only thing that changes here is the **value** of variable x. The objects 1, 5, and 6 did not change. They were just replaced.

Now, it is time for mutable objects. A list is a good example of a mutable object.

Here is an example:

```
>>> a = ["a", "b", "c"]
>>> a
['a', 'b', 'c']
>>> a.extend(['d', 'e'])
>>> a
['a', 'b', 'c', 'd', 'e']
>>> _
```

In here, instead of just reassigning a value, the list was extended. The extended list is still the same object list. Therefore, it mutated to something bigger instead of being replaced completely. To make mutability of objects much easier, it will be best to use the **id** keyword.

```
>>> id(1)
```

1730951424

```
>>> id(2)
```

1730951440

```
>>> x = 1
>>> id(x)
```

1730951424

```
>>> x = 2
>>> id(x)
```

1730951440

As you can see, the ids of objects 1 and 2 are different. And when you assign object 1 and 2 to the variable x, its id becomes the same with the object that is assigned.

Now, do this experiment with lists.

```
>>> list1 = [1, 2, 3]
>>> id(list1)
```

3491240

```
>>> list2 = [1, 2, 3, 4]
```

```
>>> id(list2)

3492400

>>> x = list1

>>> id(x)

3491240

>>> x.extend([4])

>>> x

[1, 2, 3, 4]

>>> id(x)

3491240

>>> _
```

As you can see, the id of the list [1, 2, 3] and the id of the list [1, 2, 3, 4] is different. However, the list [1, 2, 3] did not change when we extended it by adding [4] to make it similar to the list [1, 2, 3, 4]. What happened was the list was not replaced but was mutated instead.

Passing List by Value

You can use a function for passing list by value by simply using slice. For example:

```
>>> tempList = [1, 2, 3, 4]

>>> def function(mutable):

mutable += [5, 6, 7, 8]

print(mutable)
```

```
>>> function(tempList[:])
[1, 2, 3, 4, 5, 6, 7, 8]
>>> tempList
[1, 2, 3, 4]
>>> _
```

Anonymous Functions or Lambda

Using an anonymous function is a convenient way to write one-line functions that require arguments and return a value. It uses the keyword lambda. Despite having a purpose of being a one liner, it can have numerous parameters. For example: >>> average = lambda x, y, z: (x + y + z) / 3

```
>>> x = average(10, 20, 30)

>>> x

20.0

>>> average(12, 51, 231)

98.0

>>> _
```

Variable Scopes

Since global and private variables have been mentioned, this section will discuss variable scopes. There are two types of variables: global and local. Global variables are available throughout the program. When using them inside functions, you use the keyword global. In some programming languages, global variables are referred to as public variables. Local variables are only available inside a code block where it was used. The previous sections referred to it as private variables for simplification purposes. Local variables can be used by the function that declared or used it and are deleted once the function ends. For accuracy's sake, this book will now refer to global variables as global variables and local variables as local variables. Public and private variables can easily have a different connotation. And this can be confusing once you start dealing with modules.

Optional Arguments and Default Values

At this point, we know that functions require arguments to be passed to parameters. However, there are cases where you do not have an argument to pass or your arguments' values rarely deviate. In those cases, you need to use optional arguments and default values. For example: >>> def addOrMultiply(number1, number2, operation = "add"):

if (operation == "add"):

print(number1 + number2)

if (operation == "multiply"):

print(number1 * number2)

>>> addOrMultiply(12, 51)

63

>>> addOrMultiply(12, 51, "add")

63

>>> addOrMultiply(12, 51, "multiply")

612

>>> addOrMultiply(12, 51, "asld jkhb")

>>> _

Arbitrary Arguments

If you want to pass an unknown number of arguments to your function, it can be difficult to prepare parameters for them. For example, what if you want to process the names of the students who attended a certain class? The names can easily vary from one to the maximum number of students who can attend class. For that kind of scenarios, you can format your function like this:

```
>>> def classNames(*args):

 for i in range(len(args)):

 print(args[i])

>>> classNames("John", "William", "Joe")

John

William

Joe

>>> _
```

Note that ***args** indicates that the function will accept an arbitrary number of arguments. All of the arguments will be sent as items inside a tuple variable named args. When looping through the tuple args using for, you can use a variable to contain the current item being parsed inside the tuple. With that in mind, the previous example can be written as: >>> def classNames(*args):

```
 for arg in args:

 print(arg)

>>> classNames("John", "William", "Joe")
```

John

William

Joe

>>> _

You can include regular parameters inside a function that uses **args. However, note that you should place** args as the last parameter. For example: >>> def classNames(teachername, *args):

print("Teacher: " + teachername)

for i in range(len(args)):

print("Student " + str(i + 1) + ": " + args[i])

>>> classNames("Winchester", "John", "William", "Joe")

Teacher: Winchester

Student 1: John

Student 2: William

Student 3: Joe

>>> _

Also, *args are used to allow the function to accept "non-keyworded" list that will result to a tuple. You use **kwargs, on the other hand, to allow the function to accept "keyworded" list that will result to a dictionary.

Storing Functions in Modules

Writing a huge program in one file can be cumbersome. A regular program like a calculator can have hundreds of functions, and each of those functions can contain five to nine statements. If one statement equals one line of code, writing a small program with a hundred functions can make you deal with 500 to 900 lines of codes.

Even if Python is one of many programming languages revered due to its syntax' simplicity and code readability, having to find, write, and edit code in the midst of 900 lines can be tedious and confusing. When you exceed roughly 100 lines of codes or at least 10 functions, then it makes sense to use modules.

What is a module anyway? A module is simply a Python (.py) file that consists of python code. In programming, the common hierarchy is this:

Program > Modules > Functions > Statements > Variables/Expressions/Data

A program contains modules. A module contains functions. A function contains statements. A statement contains variables, expressions, data, and data. Depending on the complexity of your program, that hierarchy can easily change.

The question now is, "How to create a module?" Creating a module in Python is simple. You just need to write or paste all the functions and statements you want to be contained and save it as a *.py file. That is it. You have a new module.

Note that a module can use other modules. To use a module, you need to import them into the program using the **import** keyword. For example, here is a function inside your module. And this module will be saved as sample.py.

def sampleFunction():

print("Hello World")

```
def sampleFunction2():

 print("Hello Again")
```

Here is how to use the sampleFunction function from the sample.py module.

```
>>> import sample

>>> sample.sampleFunction()

Hello World

>>> _
```

Note that the module must be in the same directory as the program/main module (or the one importing it) for the module to be imported. If not, you will receive an error.

```
>>> import nonExistingModule

Traceback (most recent call last):

 File "<stdin>", line 1, in <module>

ModuleNotFoundError:     No     module     named
'nonExistingModule'

>>> _
```

When you use the import keyword, you will have access to all the functions inside a module. Importing a module this way will make Python treat the functions in the module as methods of the module object. In simpler terms, you will need to mention the object and use the accessor operator (.) to call the function.

If you want to use only one or a specific number of functions from the module and integrate them in the current module as if they are defined in it, you can use the **from** keyword together with import. For example: >>> from sample import sampleFunction

>>> sampleFunction()

Hello World

>>> _

You can import multiple functions by doing this:

>>> from sample import sampleFunction, sampleFunction2

>>> sampleFunction2()

Hello Again

>>> _

If you want to use the "from" keyword to get all the function from a module, you can use the asterisk or wildcard operator (*).

>>> from sample import *

>>> sampleFunction()

Hello World

>>> _

Note that you will get an error if you try to call a function without the module object and accessor if you only use import.

>>> import sample

>>> sampleFunction()

Traceback (most recent call last):

File "<stdin>", line 1, in <module>

NameError: name 'sampleFunction' is not defined

>>> _

Function and Module Styles

This section will just provide you with reminders from PEP8.

Function names should always be in lowercase, and you should separate multiple words in a function with underscores.

Remember that the styling tips and naming methods for a function are the same as those for variables.

Always follow the prevailing style in the code. If the code already follows mixed case convention, adapt to it instead of trying to change everything,

Always prevent using a function name similar to a keyword. Python is a dynamic language, and you can easily use keywords as identifiers. Use synonyms if possible.

Add a trailing underscore if a function's name is the same with a keyword, and you cannot think of an appropriate replacement. Do not corrupt the spelling. For example, use the name class_ instead of cls.

Module names should always be in lowercase. Use underscores if they can improve readability and truly needed. The same goes with Python packages.

Practice Exercises

This time, improve this basic calculator program by adding functions you can find in a scientific calculator.

Since the math module was not covered, just do away with the following features of a scientific calculator:

CMC, MR, MS, M+, M-

$\pm$

$1/x$

$10^X, x^y, x^2, x^3$

Π

Mod

Conclusion

Thank you for making it through to the end of this book. I hope it was informative and able to provide you with all of the tools you need to achieve your goals, whatever they may be. The next step is to start using some of the different topics that we have discussed in this guidebook to your advantage and learn how to work with the Python language. There are a lot of different parts that can come with this kind of coding language, and learning how they all fit together and trying out some of the different codes that are present is one of the best ways to get hands-on and ready to go with this process.

This guide spent some time taking a look at some of the different tasks that you can do with the Python language and how you can make this the right option for you. This book is meant to teach you all of the different parts that come with coding in general, but even more specifically what you are able to do with the help of this language whether you are starting as a total beginner or if you have been doing programming for a long period of time. You should find that using Python becomes easier because you already know how the program works, but with the new stuff you learned, you will be able to make more advanced moves with Python.

Once again, if you find that you are making mistakes, take the time to step back and go back and look at the stuff that you might not have understood when you went through it first. It is going to take time just like it did when you were first starting out for you to get the hang of the new techniques that you have learned.

You have already learned that programming is not going to come easy, and it is definitely not something that you are going to learn overnight. Even though Python is simple enough to use, you will be learning a whole new part of the program, and it will get more complicated the more you learn. However, you will be doing some good for yourself because you will be teaching yourself a valuable skill that can be used not only in your personal life but also in your professional life.

When you have spent some time working on the Python language, and you are ready to take your skills to the next level and develop some strong codes that can do so much in just a few lines, make sure to read through this guidebook to help you get started!

Programming is a lot like language learning. You can be a very solid speaker of a language by acting minimally, sure. But it's only by devoting yourself to a language and immersing yourself in it that you'll be able to hang with the best in terms of your ability to speak that language.

Programming is no different. If you aren't proactive, if you don't get involved in online and real-life communities and try your best to program as much as you can in as many new ways as you can find, then you're going to plateau, and you're going to plateau very, very hard.

There may be a lot of different options that you are going to work with when it is time to handle some of your biggest coding challenges. But the best one to choose is going to be Python. It has all the strength you are looking for, easy to learn and read, and much more. When you are ready to get your crash course in the Python language, and you are ready to hit the ground running, make sure to check out this guidebook to get started.

www.ingramcontent.com/pod-product-compliance
Lightning Source LLC
La Vergne TN
LVHW051742050326
832903LV00029B/2677